EDITOR-IN-CHIEF Tracy White
SPECIAL PROJECTS EDITOR Leslie Miller
ASSISTANT EDITOR Britney Mellen
SENIOR WRITER Denise Pauley
COPY EDITOR Kim Sandoval, Brittany Beattie
EDITORIAL ASSISTANTS Joannie McBride, Fred Brewer
ART DIRECTOR Brian Tippetts
DESIGNER Celeste Rockwood-Jones
PRODUCTION DESIGNERS Just Scan Me!
PRODUCTION MANAGER Gary Whitehead
FOUNDING EDITOR Lisa Bearnson
CO-FOUNDER Don Lambson

PRIMEDIA

VICE PRESIDENT, GROUP PUBLISHER David O'Neil
CIRCULATION MARKETING DIRECTORS Dena Spar, Janice Martin
PROMOTIONS DIRECTOR Dana Smith

PRIMEDIA, Inc.
CHAIRMAN Dean Nelson
PRESIDENT AND CEO Kelly Conlin
VICE-CHAIRMAN Beverly C. Chell

PRIMEDIA Enthusiast Media
EVP, CONSUMER MARKETING/CIRCULATION Steve Aster
SVP, CHIEF FINANCIAL OFFICER Kevin Neary
SVP, MFG., PRODUCTION AND DISTRIBUTION Kevin Mullan
SVP, CHIEF INFORMATION OFFICER Debra C. Robinson
VP, CONSUMER MARKETING Bobbi Gutman
VP, MANUFACTURING Gregory A. Catsaros
VP, SINGLE COPY SALES Thomas L. Fogarty
VP, MANUFACTURING BUDGETS AND OPERATIONS Lilia Golia
VP, HUMAN RESOURCES Kathleen P. Malinowski
VP, BUSINESS DEVELOPMENT Albert Messina
VP, DATABASE /E-COMMERCE Suti Prakash

PRIMEDIA Outdoor Recreation and Enthusiast Group
PRESIDENT Scott Wagner
VP, GROUP CFO Henry Donahue
VP, MARKETING AND INTERNET OPERATIONS Dave Evans

ISBN 1-929180-72-1

accents

TABLE OF
contents

accents

Everything has a star. Consider your favorite movie, outfit or meal, and chances are, one element will stand out in your mind as the most significant. But, if you give it a little more thought, you'll realize that the supporting players, the accessories and the side dishes are what make those favorites truly unforgettable.

Though your photos and journaling may take center stage on every layout, the accents surrounding them can make your pages even more memorable. The embellishments you choose, use and design are an important imprint that you leave on your layouts...a mark of your creativity and artistic vision.

Whether you lean toward flat or lumpy, handmade or premade, this book will show you some hot new techniques and cool twists to old ones that can help you create these seemingly minor elements and use them to impact your pages in a major way.

2004

April

(5)

tags and tiles

Consider them tiny canvases. Plain or painted, dyed or distressed, tags and tiles can serve as embellishments themselves or become mini mats and frames that give smaller items more visual punch.

Available in an array of styles, materials and colors, tags and tiles can be affixed to photos, borders, journaling boxes, mats and more. Attach tags with colorful ribbon and string, funky chains or shaped fasteners. Give tiles added dimension with foam tape, or add small holes to design dangling accents. Consider these projects to garner even more ideas.

ABC: by Miley Johnson
Supplies *Patterned paper:* Karen Foster Design; *Wood letters and stamp:* Mantofev; *Envelope:* FoofaLa; *Ribbon:* C.M. Offray & Son (ruler), Close To My Heart (red gingham) and Memory Lane (black stitched); *Clips:* Office Depot.

idea to note: Envelope tags are ideal for school page accents. Use them as a base for embellishments such as wood letters, notes and clips.

This is my Gr... Spohr and my ...dpa's brother, Otto. It is my absolute favorite heritage photo. Mom has it framed in her home and I have always been fascinated with this beautiful woman holding her infant son. I never knew my great grandmother, she died well before I was born. Otto died at the age of 8. **Remember**

christmas 1915

MY FAMILY, MY ROOTS

MY FAMILY, MY ROOTS: by Nichol Magouirk

Supplies *Patterned paper:* Sonnets, Creative Imaginations; *Hemp paper:* Artistic Scrapper, Creative Imaginations; *Transparency and tag:* Narratives, Creative Imaginations; *Tassel and trim:* Sonnets, Creative Imaginations; *Paint, clips, brads, staple and cream ribbon:* Making Memories; *Date rub-ons:* Art Warehouse, Creative Imaginations; *Stamping Ink:* Nick Bantock, Ranger Industries; *Other:* Silk flower and blue trim.

idea to note: To create a journaling square behind a transparency, print the text on patterned paper and adhere it behind the "frame." Lightly brush acrylic paint over the back side of the tag to create a less transparent background. Age the edges with ink.

YOU: by Nichol Magouirk
Supplies *Vellum tag and letter stickers:* Sonnets, Creative Imaginations; *Flower:* Making Memories; *Acrylic letters:* Doodlebug Design; *Rub-ons:* Art Warehouse (word) and Scrapperware (brads), Creative Imaginations; *Nailhead:* JewelCraft; *Ribbon:* Stampin' Up! (hot pink) and Making Memories (gingham and pink with white stitching); *Other:* Pin, organza and satin ribbon.

idea to note: Mix and match dimensional alphabets with alphabet stickers for a whimsical look. It's a great way to use up your stash of extra letters!

SWEET FRIEND: by Tracy Miller
Supplies *Patterned paper and die cut:* SEI; *Ribbon:* Li'l Davis Designs (pink) and SEI; *Heart stud and concho:* Scrapworks; *Pop dots:* All Night Media, Plaid Enterprises.

idea to note: Cut your own tag from patterned paper. It can serve as a visually interesting mat for a smaller accent.

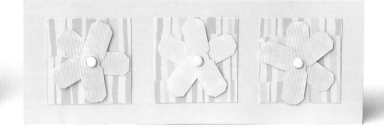

JOURNEY: by Brenda Arnall
Supplies *Rubber stamps:* Hero Arts; *Stamping ink:* StazOn, Tsukineko; *Watercolors:* Lyra; *Ceramic tile:* Collage Keepsakes, Hirschberg Schutz & Co.; *Twist tie:* Pebbles Inc.; *Washer:* Making Memories; *Gloss sealer:* Plaid Enterprises; *Other:* Vellum and fiber.

idea to note: Liven up your base by painting white ceramic tiles with watercolors before decorating.

FLOWERS: by Joy Uzarraga
Supplies *Patterned paper:* Art Warehouse, Creative Imaginations (plain) and Paperfever (patterned); *Square punch:* Marvy Uchida; *Brads:* American Tag Co.; *Tags:* Avery.

idea to note: Create small flowers by inking mini tags, use a brad to hold the "petals" together.

LEAF: by Brenda Arnall
Supplies *Patterned paper:* Pebbles Inc.; *Pen:* Zig Millennium, EK Success; *Stamping ink:* StazOn, Tsukineko; *Walnut ink:* Postmodern Design; *Rubber stamp:* Fred B. Mullett; *Wood tiles:* Litko Aerosystems; *Other:* Jute.

idea to note: Increase the richness of wood tiles with a quick wash of walnut ink.

treasure (trezĭ'er) 1. accumulated wealth 2. somethin

TREASURE: by Mellette Berezoski
Supplies *Acrylic Paint, photo corner, definition and ribbon:* Making Memories; *Stamp:* Stampin' Up!; *Embossing enamel:* Ultra Thick Embossing Enamel, Suze Weinberg for Ranger Industries; *Stamping ink:* Ranger Industries.

(12)

how to create a stamped chipboard tile:

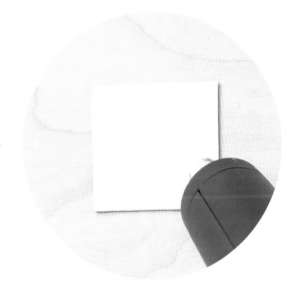

STEP 1: Paint chipboard tile and let dry.

STEP 2: Heat emboss three to four times to get a thick coating.

STEP 3: After last heat application, ink stamp with embossing ink and then press into tile.

NOEL: by Nichol Magouirk
Supplies *Tag:* Paper Reflections; *Walnut ink:* Anima
Designs; *Eyelet:* Creative Imaginations; *Staples, red
gingham ribbon, green ribbon:* Making Memories;
Folded tiles: Alphawear, Creative Imaginations; *Rub-ons:*
Scrapperware, Creative Imaginations; *Other:* Sandpaper,
ribbons and trim.

idea to note: When using folded tiles, adhere rub-ons
before folding the tiles up for easier application. Sand the
edges of the tiles after folding to age their appearance.

BABY FLASH CARDS: by Mellette Berezoski
Supplies *Computer font:* Arial Bold, Microsoft Word; *Laminate chips:* Therm
O Web; *Adhesive:* Mod Podge, Plaid Enterprises; *Ribbon:* C.M. Offray & Son;
Beaded Chain: Making Memories.

idea to note: Create a set of cute flash cards for your baby. After
they've been outgrown, remove the chain and use the cards as decorative
tags for your layouts!

scramble!

I'm not exactly sure when it started, or exactly why, but at every major event at Grandma & Pop-pop's house, we have a "candy scramble." Grandma tosses out a ton of candy and the kids, well, scramble to get as much as they can. Needless to say, Madelyn is quite motivated. You never see her move quite as fast as you see her go during a candy scramble!

may 2004

CANDY SCRAMBLE: by Tracy Miller

Supplies *Patterned paper and rub-ons:* Scrapworks; *Computer font:* Andy, Microsoft Word; *Epoxy squares:* EK Success.

idea to note: Create quick and colorful accents with epoxy squares. The self-adhesive accents can even be used as faux acrylic tiles. Or, give them a new look with stamps or rub-ons.

HULA: by Kelly Anderson
Supplies *Gold leafing pen:* Krylon; *Stamping ink:* Pinata Colors; *Other:* Dominoes and felt.

how to re-surface dominoes:

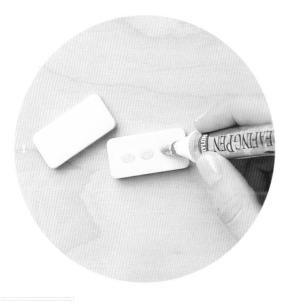

STEP 1: Using a gold leafing pen, dab three dots onto each domino.

STEP 2: Drop two to three drips of alcohol-based ink (use two to three different colors) onto a piece of felt.

STEP 3: Dab inked felt over the gold dots on the dominoes. The gold leaf pen will create an interesting effect when the colored inks are dabbed onto it.

finding accents in your photos

To give layouts a cohesive look, select embellishments that are not only an expression of the theme, but an extension of your photos. Study the following elements in each picture. Uncover little details and colors, patterns, shapes and textures that can be imitated, replicated or simply serve as a bit of design inspiration:

clothing. Can you spot any logos, T-shirt motifs, three-dimensional adornments or unique color combinations?

extras. Do any accessories or pieces of jewelry catch your eye? Do you notice buttons, zipper pulls or fasteners with an interesting shape or style? Is there a toy, a purse or other items that you can single out?

surroundings. Is your subject sitting near colorful flowers, collecting shells on the beach, participating in a sporting event, showing off a prized possession or playing happily with beloved toys?

CELEBRATE: by Denise Pauley
Supplies *Textured paper:* Books by Hand; *Patterned paper:* KI Memories; *Tiles:* The Paper Magic Group; *Stamps:* Hero Arts; *Stamping ink:* VersaMagic, Tsukineko.

idea to note: Raid your child's stash of letter tiles and create your own acrylic accents...cover the letters with patterned paper, stamped images and more.

LOVE, LAUGH: by Denise Pauley
Supplies *Patterned paper:* Sonnets, Creative Imaginations and Scenic Route Paper Co.; *Microscope slides:* FoofaLa; *Stamp:* Hero Arts; *Stamping ink:* StazOn, Tsukineko; *Ribbon:* Making Memories.

idea to note: Plastic microscope slides can be painted, stamped and layered just like their glass counterparts...but they can also be punched and strung with less danger of shattering.

MJ: by Joy Uzarraga

Supplies *Patterned paper and stickers:* Scrappy Cat Creations; *Acrylic paints:* Delta Technical Coatings; *Aluminum tags:* Anima Designs; *Rubber stamp:* Penny Black, Inc.; *Paper flower:* Making Memories; *Ribbon:* Bucilla.

 idea to note: Before applying acrylic paint to the aluminum tag, sand it to help the paint adhere. Stamp while the paint is still wet. The image will appear as the paint is lifted off the tag and onto the stamp. Clean the stamp before pressing again.

HALLOWEEN SPOOK: by Kelly Anderson

Supplies *Patterned paper:* Paper Reflections; *Mesh and metal letter:* Making Memories; *Tag:* Avery; *Label stickers:* Pebbles Inc.; *Other:* Brads, definition, metal-rimmed tag and negative strips.

idea to note: Trim a definition to fit inside a metal-rimmed tag to serve as a sleek framed accent.

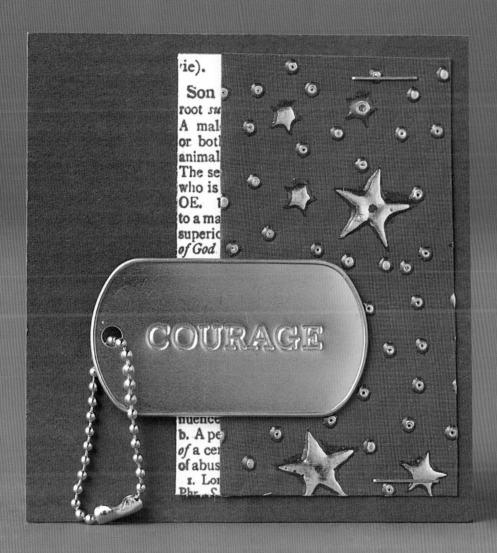

COURAGE: by Jamie Waters
Supplies *Patterned paper*: K & Company; *Textured paper*: Artistic Scrapper, Creative Imaginations; *Dog tag and beaded chain*: Li'l Davis Designs; *Staples*: Making Memories.

idea to note: Make a statement with pre-embossed metal dog tags, or start with blank versions and design your own with metal stamps.

frames
and frills

Thin, gold edging. A length of silk ribbon. A swatch of luxurious velvet. An understated silver frame. With just a bit of texture and depth, little frames and touches of ribbon or fabric can add both elegance and a hint of femininity to your layouts.

Whether you're enclosing small photos, tiny accents, snippets of journaling or memorabilia, a frame is the perfect way to add emphasis and interest to your page. And with a dash of ribbon, fabric or flowers, most any layout can take an immediate turn from basic to beautiful. But don't be fooled—these dainty accents can be adapted for funky and even masculine looks. Discover their versatility in the following layouts and projects.

APRIL: by Shannon Wolz
Supplies *Ticket:* Li'l Davis Designs; *Tag, flower, brad and rub-ons:* Making Memories; *Stamping ink:* Ranger Industries; *Button:* Junkitz; *Beads:* Beadies, AIC; *Square punch:* EK Success; *Other:* Ribbon and string.

idea to note: A metal-rimmed tag makes a perfect mini frame. Boost the accent's glitz by adhering a photo to the tag, then layering rub-on words, adhesive and micro beads on top for sparkle.

INFRARED: by Brenda Arnall

Supplies *Patterned paper:* Chatterbox; *Specialty Paper:* Sam Flax; *Computer fonts:* Maszyna (title) and My Type of Font (journaling), downloaded from the Internet; *Stamping ink:* ColorToolBox, Clearsnap; *Pen:* Zig Millennium, EK Success; *Slide mounts:* Scrapworks; *Ribbon:* Making Memories; *Label maker:* Dymo; *Other:* Picture hanger, string and negative strip.

idea to note: In addition to serving as small frames, slide mounts can also become covers for clever mini books to hold small photos, memorabilia and more.

DAISIES DADDY: by Joy Uzarraga
Supplies: *Rubber stamp:* Dawn Houser, Inkadinkado; *Stamping ink:* Memories, Stewart Superior Corporation; *Silk flowers:* Teters.

idea to note: Placed at the corner of your accent, large silk flowers add color and help show off smaller photos and embellishments.

SENIOR YEAR: by Kelly Anderson
Supplies *Patterned paper and label sticker:* Li'l Davis Designs; *Frame:* Making Memories; *Alphabet stamps:* PSX Design; *Stamping ink:* Brilliance, Tsukineko; *Acrylic paint:* Delta Technical Coatings; *Letters:* Paper Bliss; *Ribbon:* Marvy Uchida; *Pen:* Zig Millennium, EK Success.

idea to note: Letter tiles make ideal dimensional monograms for smaller pieces.

[2], to regard with affec
affecti e (lŭv) [2],
HOPE
loves lovely (lŭv′lĭ)

You are the hope in my life.

HOPE: by Mellette Berezoski
Supplies *Patterned paper:* The Scrapbook Wizard (floral), Scrapworks (stripe) and K & Company (words); *Conchos:* Scrapworks; *Letter stickers:* The Scrapbook Wizard; *Hinge and ribbon:* Making Memories.

idea to note: Create a quick frame for a tiny photo and accents with conchos. (*Note:* To keep your photo in place, adhere it to the background first, then press the concho down around it.)

BABY: by Miley Johnson
Supplies *Tag and brads:* Making Memories; *Alphabet stamps:* PSX Design; *Stamping ink:* Close To My Heart; *Other:* Paper doily, flowers and ribbon.

idea to note: Fashion a gorgeous corner accent by cutting a doily in half, then folding it in half again. Adorn it with embellishments such as flowers and an embossed monogram tag.

REMEMBER THIS: by Mellette Berezoski
Supplies *Patterned paper:* 7gypsies; *Handmade paper:* Magic Scraps; *Pressed flowers:* Pressed Petals; *Microscope slide:* FoofaLa; *Rub-ons, ribbon, and photo corner:* Making Memories; *Metal word tag:* K & Company.

idea to note: For a beautiful and natural flourish, use pressed flowers or leaves to dress up your accent.

BASEBALL: by Nichol Magouirk
Supplies *Negative sleeves:* Narratives, Creative Imaginations; *Stickers:* Karen Foster Design; *Washer and eyelet:* Making Memories; *Other:* Hemp.

idea to note: Cut apart negative sleeves and hang them for a cool vertical look. Use the mini frames to showcase memorabilia, small photos and other embellishments.

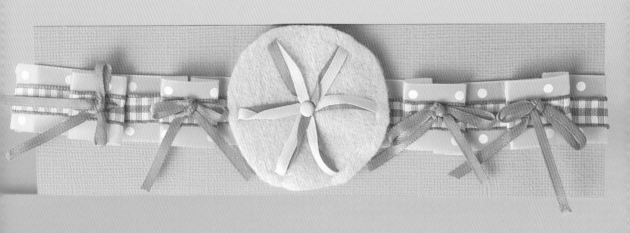

GARTER: by Miley Johnson
Supplies *Ribbon:* C.M. Offray & Son (yellow dot, yellow and pink solid) and Close To My Heart (pink gingham); *Felt:* Michaels; *Brad:* Lasting Impressions for Paper.

how to create
ribbon ruffles:

STEP 1: Adhere gingham ribbon to dotted ribbon. Create a pleat about an inch wide.

STEP 2: Using a large sewing needle, thread thin ribbon through the pleat, leaving the two ends on top.

STEP 3: Secure ends with a bow.

STEP 4: Repeat steps 1-4 along the length of the ribbon and attach to felt backing.

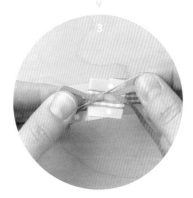

SWEET ONE: by Kelly Anderson
Supplies *Canvas and pins:* Li'l Davis Designs; *Other:* Rickrack.

idea to note: Rickrack, blanket banding and other decorative trims can add a sweet touch to baby accents.

MEMORIES: by Denise Pauley
Supplies *Specialty paper:* Maruyama, Magenta; *Flowers, ribbon and stamp:* Making Memories; *Stamping ink:* StazOn (black) and VersaMagic (white and pink), Tsukineko; *Tag:* Avery.

idea to note: Knots give flower centers added dimension and character as well as doubling as fasteners. To create one, knot a piece of ribbon, thread both ends through the flower's center and the cardstock and secure in back with tape.

MEGAN: by Joy Uzarraga
Photo by Cherie Wayne. Supplies *Patterned paper:* KI Memories; *Stamps:* Hero Arts; *Stamping ink:* Memories, Stewart Superior Corporation; *Ribbon:* May Arts (polka dot) and Making Memories (pink); *Flowers:* Making Memories; *Brads:* The Happy Hammer; *Hole reinforcements:* Target; *Other:* Lace.

idea to note: A touch of lace is a textbook accent to highlight pretty photos. Use it to adorn tags, titles and mats.

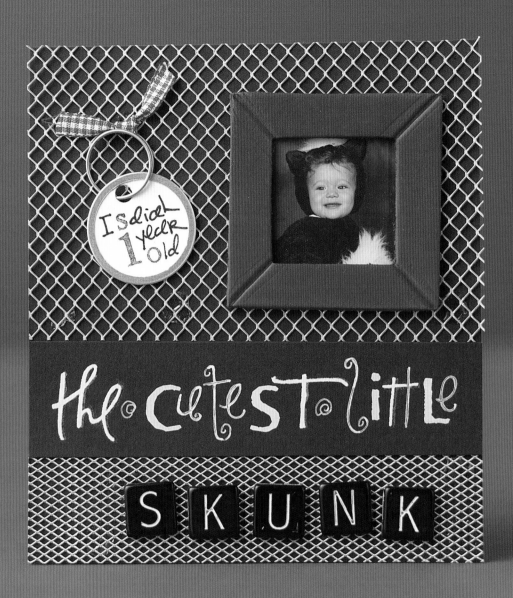

LITTLE SKUNK: by Kelly Anderson
Supplies *Leather frame, rub-ons and mesh:* Making Memories; *Letters:* Paper Bliss; *Alphabet stamps:* PSX Design; *Stamping ink:* Brilliance, Tsukineko; *Ribbon:* Midori; *Pens:* Gel Roller, Marvy Uchida (white) and Zig Millennium, EK Success (black); *Tag:* Avery.

idea to note: Colorful leather frames can help highlight a focal photo on your accent block.

BE HAPPY: by Denise Pauley

Supplies *Fabric:* Artistic Scrapper, Creative Imaginations; *Patterned paper:* Autumn Leaves; *Corrugated cardstock:* DMD, Inc.; *Glass enclosure:* Pebbles Inc.; *Stamps:* Making Memories (flourish) and Hero Arts (sentiment); *Stamping ink:* StazOn, Tsukineko (black) and Fresco, Stampa Rosa (blue); *Envelope tag:* Anima Designs; *Twill tape:* Creekbank Creations; *Pressed flowers:* Colorbök; *Beads:* Darice.

idea to note: Dimensional mini frames can be turned into shakers that hold photos, flowers, beads, shells, sand, glitter and more.

W&B: by Brenda Arnall

Supplies *Patterned paper:* Paper Adventures; *Specialty paper:* Magenta; *Corrugated paper:* DMD, Inc.; *Rubber stamps:* Hero Arts; *Stamping ink:* ColorToolBox, Clearsnap, and StazOn, Tsukineko; *Pen:* Zig Millennium, EK Success; *Label holder:* Magic Scraps; *Metal letters:* Making Memories; *Cork tag:* Artistic Scrapper, Creative Imaginations; *Gold leafing pen:* Krylon; *Acrylic paint:* Golden Artist Colors; *Other:* Vellum, jute and ticket.

idea to note: In addition to enclosing text, label holders make great decorative frames for tiny photos.

I MISS YOU: by Jamie Waters
Supplies *Die cut*: KI Memories; *Watch crystal*: Scrapworks; *Alphabet stamps*: PSX Design; *Ribbon*: Li'l Davis Designs; *Other*: Stamping ink.

how to create a watch crystal photo frame:

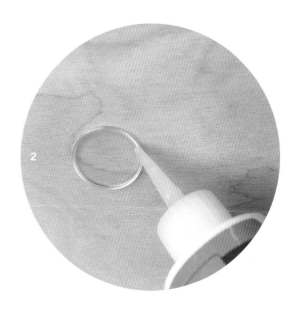

STEP 1: Attach photo to die cut.

STEP 2: Use glue pen (or other liquid adhesive) to draw a thin line of glue around the back edge of the crystal. *(Note:* Avoid applying too much glue, as it will ooze as you press the crystal over the photo.)

STEP 3: Turn the crystal over and carefully place over photo. Hold for a moment to allow glue to set.

the little things

Ever feel like your layout is missing something? Though the photos are expressive, the journaling flawless and the color and composition beyond compare, you may still believe your page needs more oomph. Luckily, all it requires is some decorative detail to take it from "well..." to "wow!"

With a touch of beading, for example, a simple stitched border gains eye-catching dimension and pizzazz. And with a bit of sequined trim, a small stamped image suddenly finds itself a glamorous wedding accent. You're already going to great lengths to create memorable pages...why not take the extra step to make them grand? Read on, and you may just be inspired by these little accents that can have a big impact on the stylishness of your designs.

TO HAVE AND TO HOLD: by Joy Uzarraga
Supplies *Rub-on phrase:* Making Memories; *Sequined trim:* Hobby Lobby; *Rubber stamp:* A Muse Artstamps; *Stamping ink:* Versamark, Tsukineko; *Chalk:* Craf-T Products.

idea to note: For a soft image, stamp with embossing ink, then lightly add chalk over the impression, building up color until the desired tone is achieved.

YUM: by Jamie Waters
Supplies *Patterned paper and die cut:* KI Memories; *Rub-ons:* Scrapworks; *Ribbon:* Li'l Davis Designs (green); *Tag:* Avery; *Other:* Letter beads and pink ribbon.

idea to note: Colorful alphabet beads can add a whimsical touch to accents for kid pages.

DADDY'S GIRL: by Mellette Berezoski
Supplies *Patterned paper:* Bo Bunny Press; *Beads:* Magic Scraps; *Fabric:* Junkitz; *Tags, wire and stick-pins:* Making Memories.

idea to note: A hand-beaded border can make an already colorful embellishment pop by adding attention-grabbing dimension.

Maysie & Dayton - July - 2004

together

COMFY COZY

ADORE

happiness

HUGS

I hope you always know how truly lucky you are to have each other ♥ Mom

HUGS: by Mellette Berezoski
Supplies *Patterned paper, flowers and bookplate:* KI Memories; *Tags and brads:* Making Memories; *Woven label:* me & my BIG ideas; *Ribbon:* C.M. Offray & Son and Making Memories.

idea to note: Small acrylic flowers scattered across your background will enhance the color and tenderness of your layout.

HUSBAND: by Miley Johnson
Supplies *Alphabet stamps, definition and ribbon:* FoofaLa; *Key:* Li'l Davis Designs; *Stamp:* Inkadinkadoo; *Stamping ink:* Nick Bantock, Ranger Industries; *Ribbon:* Memory Lane; *Other:* Burlap.

idea to note: Does your husband hold the key to your heart? Show it by adorning your page with a classic metal key.

DREAM: by Jamie Waters
Supplies *Vellum and die cut:* KI Memories; *Washer and brad:* Making Memories; *Other:* Eyelets and ribbon.

idea to note: Use an engraved washer as the centerpiece of your simple, geometric accent.

"A": by Shannon Wolz
Supplies *Letter gem accent:* Gap Kids; *Circle punch:* EK Success; *Ribbon and jump ring:* Making Memories; *Stamping ink:* ColorToolBox, Clearsnap.

idea to note: Use tiny gems, sequins, buttons or studs to add sparkle to small accents. Find premade gem monograms that can easily be adhered to cardstock.

CREATE LOVE: by Mellette Berezoski
Supplies *Patterned paper:* 7gypsies (black) and Wordsworth (pink); *Acrylic tokens:* Doodlebug Design; *Stickers:* Making Memories; *Other:* Decorative trim.

idea to note: Use acrylic tokens etched with cute images to add interest to your accent block.

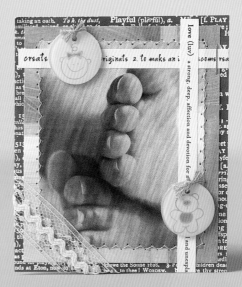

BE MINE: by Nichol Magouirk
Supplies *Ribbon (red), jump rings, pin and rub-ons:* Making Memories; *Glass bottle:* K & Company; *Tags:* Paper Reflections and Making Memories; *Walnut ink:* Anima Designs; *Eyelet:* Creative Imaginations; *Gel medium:* Liquitex; *Decoupage glaze:* Mod Podge, Plaid Enterprises; *Other:* Ribbon (black).

customize glass bottles with image transfer:

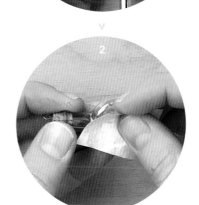

STEP 1: Print a contact print in reverse on a plain sheet of paper and trim.

STEP 2: Apply a very thin layer of gel medium to the flat surface of the glass with your finger. Lay photo over medium and burnish.

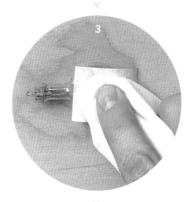

STEP 3: Wet a soft cloth and gently blot paper until damp.

STEP 4: Gently remove paper from bottle.

(43)

SKYLINE: by Joy Uzarraga
Photo by Ronald Uzarraga. Supplies *Slide mount:* DMD, Inc.; *Sea glass:* Magic Scraps; *Embroidery floss:* Making Memories; *Stamping ink:* ColorToolBox, Clearsnap.

idea to note: Bits of sea glass can become a colorful corner that adds impact to smaller photo accents.

NOMAD: by Tracy Miller
Supplies *Patterned paper, epoxy words and frames:* Li'l Davis Designs; *Vellum quote:* Memories Complete; *Ribbon:* SEI.

idea to note: To support the theme of your layout, layer a vellum quote over a patterned paper with a complementary design.

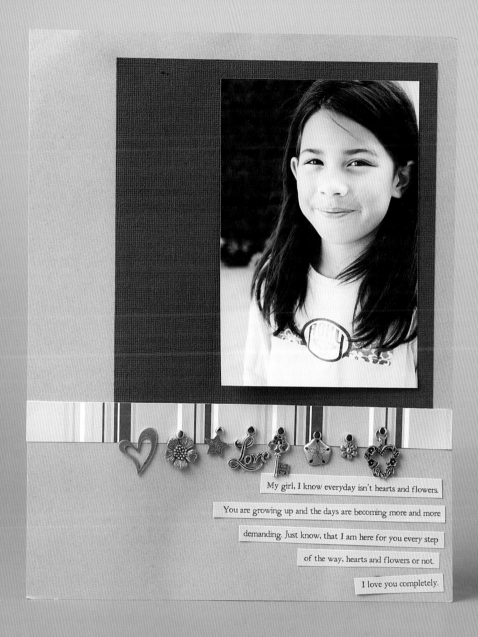

My girl, I know everyday isn't hearts and flowers.

You are growing up and the days are becoming more and more

demanding. Just know, that I am here for you every step

of the way, hearts and flowers or not.

I love you completely.

HEARTS AND FLOWERS: by Jamie Waters
Supplies *Patterned papers:* Scrapworks; *Computer font:* Butterbrotpapier, downloaded from the Internet; *Other:* Charms and brads.

idea to note: For an eye-catching, classic touch, adorn a strip of patterned paper with assorted pewter charms.

setting the tone with accents

While your photos dictate the subject of each layout, your embellishments can further the theme. Accents with a specific style do more than just establish the feel of your layout, they can also support your photos and enhance the mood and memories they evoke. Depending on the desired tone, take the following additions into consideration:

elegant and elaborate.
Think heavy fabrics, matte metals, ornate corners, pewter stickers, metallic rub-ons or leaf flakes.

funky and playful.
Try hand-painted accents, acrylic shapes, buttons, colorful punch outs or items dangling on chains or string.

masculine and outdoorsy.
Create with denim, wood tiles, metal mesh, pressed leaves, subdued woven labels or color washes.

sweet and serene.
Use flowers, delicate beads, sequins, chalks, watercolors, toile, gauze or flannel.

GIRL STUFF: by Nichol Magouirk
Supplies *Patterned paper:* SEI; *Alphabet stamps:* Ma Vinci's Reliquary; *Conchos:* Scrapworks (frame, squares), JewelCraft (round) and K & Company (round with word); *Ribbon:* Sweetwater; *Brad:* Scrapperware, Creative Imaginations.

idea to note: Conchos can serve as frames and fasteners. They can even take the place of small buckles. To create a file folder, trace a mini file folder onto patterned paper before hand cutting.

TIME IN A BOTTLE: by Kelly Anderson
Supplies *Alphabet stamps:* PSX Design; *Watch faces and bottle:* K & Company; *Watch parts:* www.lasioux.com; *Pin:* Li'l Davis Designs; *Stamping ink:* Brilliance, Tsukineko (black) and Stampa Rosa (brown); *Pen:* Zig Millennium, EK Success.

idea to note: Watch parts are always a cool little detail for time-related accent blocks, adding shine and a hint of dimension.

POSTCARD: by Kelly Anderson
Supplies *Mesh fabric:* Ink It!; *Stickers:* Nostalgiques, EK Success; *Other:* Shell necklace.

idea to note: Give a tropical feel to travel page embellishments by adding a few small shells.

SWEET DREAMS: by Brenda Arnall
Supplies *Patterned paper:* KI Memories; *Pen:* Zig Millennium, EK Success; *Rub-ons:* Scrapworks; *Tags:* Making Memories; *Micro beads:* Beadies, AIC; *Heart charms:* JewelCraft; *Ribbons and fiber:* Sam Flax (blue and white), Wrights (rickrack) and DMC (string).

how to create beaded accents:

STEP 1: Cut small pieces of red liner tape to fill star-shaped tags (tape strips can overlap slightly, as long as the entire shape is covered).

STEP 2: Place your tag in a bead tray or on a paper plate. Remove the red liner leaving a sticky surface on the tag. Cover with beads.

premade (pretty much)

There was a time when "premade accents" always meant stickers or the occasional perforated die cut. And though the stigma of "plain" or "overly cute" often remains, cutting-edge scrapbookers realize that not only have these accents evolved—for the better—over time, but that they can also be customized to suit any need.

Save time by using a photo-realistic punchout tags or stickers. Cut work in half by applying a preprinted die cut, woven label or vellum quote. You'll be amazed at the results...and all the effort you've escaped. If you're in a really crafty mood, these embellishments can also be the starting point for more advanced looks. Examine the following projects to see how premade accents can be layered, texturized, colored, distressed and more.

EAT CAKE: by Tracy Miller
Supplies *Woven label:* me & my BIG ideas; *Sticker:* Pebbles Inc.; *Studs and Wax floss:* Scrapworks; *Other:* Jute.

idea to note: Make a quick, cute accent with a photo-realistic sticker and a woven label. For a birthday theme, use colored studs to mimic sprinkles on a cake.

NATURE: by Brenda Arnall

Supplies *Patterned paper:* Sonnets, Creative Imaginations (blue background) and Autumn Leaves (pastel pattern); *Pewter stickers:* Magenta; *Acrylic paint:* Golden Artist Colors and Liquitex; *Metal molding and letters:* Making Memories; *Gold leafing pen:* Krylon; *Other:* Fibers.

idea to note: Give pewter stickers an antiqued finish by coating them with a gold leafing pen and brushing them with acrylic paint.

FOR YOU: by Jamie Waters

Supplies *Patterned paper, conchos and punch out words:* Scrapworks; *Stamping ink:* Memories, Stewart Superior Corporation.

idea to note: Add text easily and stylishly to accents with preprinted cardstock punch outs. Frame them with conchos for a more finished look.

CLING TO WORTHY FRIENDS: by Shannon Wolz

Supplies *Patterned paper, letter and tag stickers:* Pebbles Inc.; *Computer font:* Typewriter New Roman, downloaded from the Internet; *Quote stickers:* My Mind's Eye and Making Memories; *Stamping ink:* Ranger Industries; *Other:* Ribbon, eyelets and staples.

idea to note: A quote sticker can sum up everything your photos represent. Alter plain stickers to suit your layout's color with chalks, paints or a wash of walnut ink.

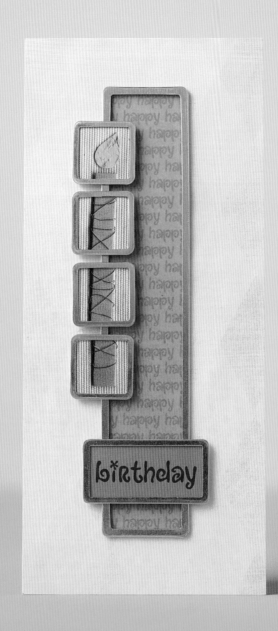

HAPPY BIRTHDAY: by Brenda Arnall
Supplies *Patterned paper:* K & Company; *Computer font:* Bohemian Garden Party, downloaded from the Internet; *Die cuts:* Fresh Cuts, EK Success;
Metal-rimmed tags: Making Memories; *Acrylic paint:* Liquitex; *Other:* Vellum.

idea to note: Preprinted die cuts can be trimmed to fit inside metal-rimmed tags for a mosaic-style accent.

I DO: by Denise Pauley
Supplies *Textured paper:* Artistic Scrapper, Creative Imaginations; *Letter stickers:* ScrapPagerz.com; *Photo stickers:* Pebbles Inc.; *Stamping ink:* Fresco, Stampa Rosa; *Photo corners:* Embellish It!, Boutique Trims; *Ribbon:* C.M. Offray & Son; *Other:* Silk flower.

idea to note: Add interest to photo-realistic stickers by sanding the edges, stringing them together and increasing their dimension with foam tape.

HIS AND MINE: by Jamie Waters
Supplies *Patterned paper and clips:* Scrapworks; *Rub-ons:* Making Memories; *Vellum quote:* Memories Complete; *Corner rounder:* Marvy Uchida.

idea to note: A vellum quote makes an easy and elegant overlay for a small photo.

CELEBRATE: by Miley Johnson
Supplies *Stickers:* Jolee's Boutique (ladybug) and Nostalgiques, EK Success (number); *Rub-ons:* Making Memories; *Ribbon:* C.M. Offray & Son; *Brad:* Magic Scraps; *Other:* Twill.

idea to note: Even dimensional stickers can receive additional adornment with charms, photos or smaller stickers.

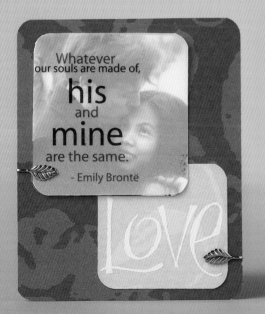

shopping
eQuals
happiness

SHOPPING EQUALS HAPPINESS: by Tracy Miller
Supplies *Patterned paper:* Making Memories; *Laser die cut:* Deluxe Designs; *Die cut and concho:* Scrapworks; *Pen:* Marvy Uchida; *Other:* Ribbon.

(56)

how to custom color laser die cuts:

STEP 1: Trace die cut onto dark cardstock. Cut around the outside edge.

STEP 2: Apply masking tape to the parts of the die cut that you want to keep the original color. Use a low-tack tape and do not adhere firmly. Use a felt-tipped pen to color the remainder of the die cut. When ink has dried, remove masking tape.

STEP 3: Adhere cardstock to die cut with liquid adhesive.

OUR TRAVELS: by Tracy Miller
Supplies *Die cuts:* Sweetwater; *Letter stickers:* me & my BIG ideas; *Index tabs:* 7gypsies; *Conchos:* Scrapworks; *Stamping ink:* Distress Ink, Ranger Industries; *Other:* Label strips.

idea to note: Get realistic textured and stitched looks in a fraction of the time by using preprinted die cuts.

LIVIN' IT UP: by Tracy Miller
Supplies *Tag:* Waste Not Paper; *Stickers:* SEI; *Rub-ons:* Li'l Davis Designs.

idea to note: Border stickers don't always have to run the length of your layouts—trim them to add a dash of color to smaller accents.

GRANDPARENTS: by Denise Pauley
Supplies *Patterned paper and punch outs:* KI Memories; *Stamping ink:* Nick Bantock, Ranger Industries; *Ribbon:* K & Company; *Staples and mesh eyelets:* Making Memories; *Other:* Thread.

idea to note: Preprinted cardstock punch outs can be tailored to any layout. Try stamping, punching, sewing, crumpling, sanding or coloring them.

FLOWER: by Shannon Wolz
Supplies *Sticker:* O'Scrap!; *Stamping ink:* Making Memories.

how to re-color and add height to stickers:

STEP 1: Mount sticker on chipboard and cut around the outside of the sticker.

STEP 2: Rub a brown ink pad over sticker for an aged look.

no accents in your color?
no problem!

If you're a late-night scrapper, you know how annoying it is to be on the verge of finishing a layout only to discover that you need green ribbon when the sole shade in your stash is white. Don't fret, because in this age of altering, it's easier than ever to re-color accents to suit your needs. Think about these options:

paints. Acrylic paints can instantly change the face of metals, acrylics, cardstock and more. In addition, watercolors can give cardstock punch outs and patterned paper accents a subtle new tint.

dyes and color washes. Ribbon, strings, fabric or cardstock can be dipped, brushed or spritzed with dye to take on an entirely new hue.

inks. A few swipes from an ink pad can change an item's color and its texture with a bit of stippling.

rub-ons. Add instant elegance and a metallic sheen with a swirl of rub-ons.

chalk. With a swipe of chalk, machine stitching, die cuts, twill tape and more, you can receive soft, updated color.

TRUE LOVE: by Denise Pauley
Supplies *Textured paper:* Provo Craft (red textured) and Black Ink (handmade); *Stickers:* Pebbles Inc.; *Stencil:* Ma Vinci's Reliquary; *Stamping ink:* Distress Ink, Ranger Industries; *Pebble and brads:* Making Memories; *Letter beads and jute:* Darice; *Other:* Playing card.

idea to note: Premade cardstock sticker tags can be layered, knotted and strung just like the real thing. They don't even require any additional adhesive to stick!

J&M: by Mellette Berezoski
Supplies *Tags:* Pebbles Inc. (round dictionary), K & Company (butterfly), The Paper Loft (flower), Li'l Davis Designs, and Creative Imaginations (burlap); *Alphabet stickers:* Creative Imaginations (black) and K & Company (brown); *Metal heart:* Carolee's Creations; *Button:* Making Memories; *Ribbon:* Li'l Davis Designs (dotted tan), Making Memories (tan and black) and SEI (blue); *Rivet:* Chatterbox; *Other:* Jute, brad.

idea to note: Experiment with mixing and matching accents to create your own beautiful and eclectic designs. This accent uses premade tags from four different sets.

FASHIONISTA: by Kelly Anderson
Supplies *Belt stickers:* Memories Complete; *Letter stickers:* SEI.

idea to note: Trim border stickers to desired size for a custom background.

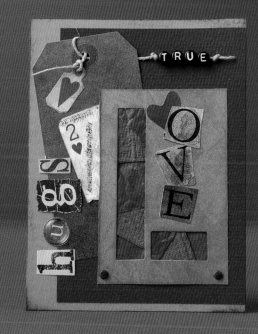

artistic touches

Sometimes you feel like getting your hands dirty and enjoying a creative process. Sometimes you just want to try out some new "stuff" in the hopes of garnering a host of colorful, textured, eye-catching looks. And sometimes, all it takes to produce the perfect accent is a medium, an idea and a little experimentation.

Show off a little shine with glazes and glues. Boost dimension with a bit of embossing powder. Increase texture with modeling paste. Or, enhance color with inks, washes and rub-ons. It's imaginative, it's easy and, most of all, it's fun. Here are numerous ways to add a hint of handmade artistry to your accents.

ART: by Miley Johnson

Supplies *Metal stamps and tag:* FoofaLa; *Metal letters:* Making Memories; *Twill:* 7gypsies; *Ribbon:* Memory Lane; *Stamp:* Inkadinkado; *Brads:* Lasting Impressions for Paper.

idea to note: Give accents a cool tie-dyed appearance by embossing images in white and coating them with a quick watercolor wash.

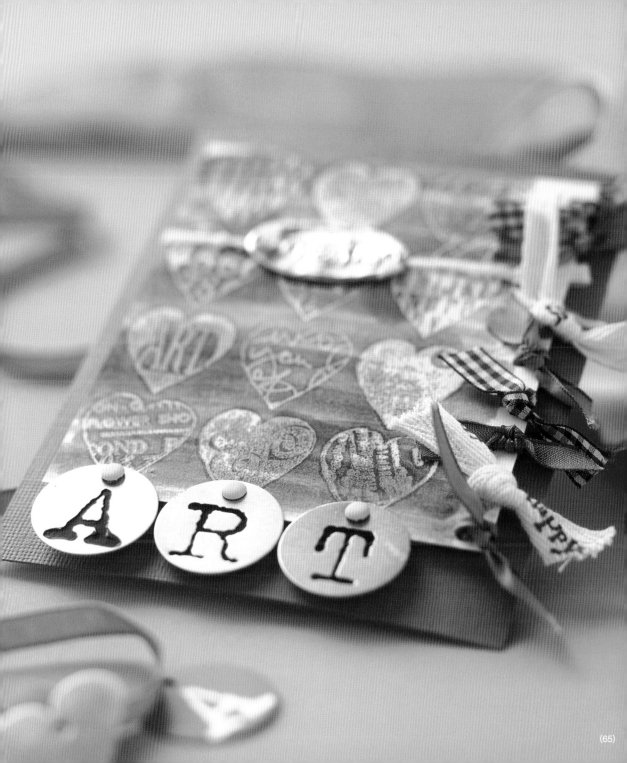

SOULS: by Tracy Miller
Supplies *Computer font:* Garamond, Microsoft Word; *Stamps:* Vicki Enkoff; *Circle punch:* McGill; *Stamping ink:* Petal Point, Colorbök.

idea to note: To create easy accents with a textured finish, stamp cardstock with pigment ink, then punch it into circles and adhere it to dark cardstock.

THANK YOU: by Jamie Waters
Supplies *Watercolors:* RoseArt; *Woven label:* me & my BIG ideas.

idea to note: Apply watercolors to fashion quick multi-hued backgrounds. Allow colors to run a little to achieve pretty blends.

HULA AT THE LUAU: by Kelly Anderson

Supplies *Patterned paper:* Scrapworks; *Gel medium:* Golden Artist Colors; *Alphabet stamps:* PSX Design; *Stamping ink:* Brilliance, Tsukineko; *Pen:* Zig Millennium, EK Success; *Other:* Mesh, tags and travel memorabilia.

idea to note: Let gel medium pull double duty—employ it as an adhesive to affix travel memorabilia to a row of tags, and once it's set, add an additional layer over the top for a glossy finish.

BELIEVE: by Mellette Berezoski

Supplies *Patterned paper:* Paper Adventures (snowflakes), Colorbök (gingham) and Creative Imaginations (dark blue); *Wooden snowflake:* Walnut Hollow; *Rub-on word:* Making Memories; *Decoupage glaze:* Mod Podge, Plaid Enterprises; *Ribbon:* C.M. Offray & Son; *Other:* Thread.

idea to note: Use decoupage glaze to adhere the patterned paper pieces to the wood accent, then coat with a second layer before adding the rub-on word.

LAUGHTER...: by Brenda Arnall
Supplies *Acrylic paint:* Liquitex; *Pen:* Zig Millennium, EK Success; *Rub-ons and ribbon:* Making Memories; *Charm:* JewelCraft; *Other:* Sheet music.

idea to note: For a background with beautiful depth and detail, scan sheet music, print it on colored cardstock, and cover it with a wash of acrylic paint.

BIRTHDAY PARTY: by Kelly Anderson
Supplies *Chalk:* Craf-T Products; *Colored pencils:* EK Success; *Pen:* Zig Millennium, EK Success.

idea to note: Pull out your pens, chalks and colored pencils to design page accents. Use text and playful colors...you're only limited by your own imagination!

TOGETHERNESS: by Joy Uzarraga
Supplies *Tag:* Artistic Scrapper, Creative Imaginations; *Stamps:* Hampton Art Stamps ("U") and Hero Arts; *Chalk and metallic rub-ons:* Craf-T Products; *Sticker:* Making Memories; *Other:* Hot glue.

idea to note: Design faux seals by dispensing a quarter-sized amount of hot glue onto a piece of cardstock. Press stamp immediately into the glue, allow it to cool for a minute, then carefully remove the stamp. Apply rub-ons for a metallic finish, then trim the cardstock around the shape.

SOAR: by Denise Pauley
Supplies *Specialty paper:* Maruyama, Magenta; *Stamps:* Rubber Stampede; *Pen:* Staedtler; *Stamping ink:* StazOn, Tsukineko and Adirondack, Ranger Industries; *Brads, eyelet and string:* Making Memories; *Dimensional adhesive:* JudiKins; *Other:* Fabric, silver paint and thread.

how to create faux pewter accents:

STEP 1: Spread dimensional glue evenly over cardstock. Allow to dry until tacky.

STEP 2: Coat stamp with clear embossing ink (to prevent sticking) and press into glue. Remove and wash stamp immediately.

STEP 3: Trim image to desired size and paint with a thin coat of pewter acrylic paint.

living with lumpy elements

Though you love the look of those big round beads, uber-dimensional bottle caps or thick wood tiles, it's understandable to be concerned about the damage their height and rigidity might cause. But with a little planning, it's easy to incorporate items of maximum dimension with minimal risk. Try the following:

Don't overcrowd your albums, and be sure to store them upright. If layouts have room to breathe and aren't smashed together for posterity, bulky accents are unlikely to leave impressions on facing pages.

Create a shadow box. Use chipboard, popdots or foam tape to build a frame for dimensional elements (or your entire page), allowing them to recede. Facing pages will press against the flat frame, rather than against the oddly shaped accent. Want another option? Select a page protector created from rigid plastic that's designed to encase layouts featuring bulky items.

Recreate the look. With a little experimentation, most accents can be replicated in flat, forgiving versions. Wood veneer, for example, can be punched and raised with foam tape to look like thick wood pieces, while metal sheets can be shaped, embossed and de-bossed to look like fasteners, plaques, dog tags, frames and more.

HAPPY BIRTHDAY: by Joy Uzarraga
Supplies *Texture paste:* Liquitex; *Gems:* Westrim Crafts; *Beads:* me & my BIG ideas; *Stamp:* Savvy Stamps; *Stamping ink:* Fluid Chalk, Clearsnap; *Ribbon:* C.M. Offray & Son.

NATURAL: by Nichol Magouirk
Supplies *Stencil:* Autumn Leaves; *Embossing enamel:* Ultra Thick Embossing Enamel, Suze Weinberg for Ranger Industries; *Stamping ink:* Nick Bantock, Ranger Industries; *Skeletal leaves:* Golden Oak Papers; *Pressed flowers:* Pressed Petals; *Staples and ribbon:* Making Memories; *Fabric:* Junkitz.

idea to note: Achieve this look by adding several layers of embossing enamel to the stencil and carefully embedding the skeletal leaves and pressed flower while it's still hot. Add two more layers of embossing enamel to firmly adhere the items.

LIFE'S JOURNEY: by Jamie Waters
Supplies *Patterned paper:* K & Company; *Transparency:* Narratives, Creative Imaginations; *Foil:* Reynolds; *Acrylic paint and staples:* Making Memories; *Bookplate:* Li'l Davis Designs; *Stickers:* me & my BIG ideas.

idea to note: Design an embossed accent with aluminum foil. Place foil on top of an embossed metal accent, use a popsicle stick to dry emboss the design onto the foil, then use a bit of paint to give the image further definition after trimming.

FEELIN' GROOVY: by Tracy Miller
Supplies *Tags:* SEI; *Gold leafing pen:* Krylon; *Studs and rub-on letters:* Scrapworks.

idea to note: Up the glitz on your page by tracing over designs on premade accents with a leafing pen.

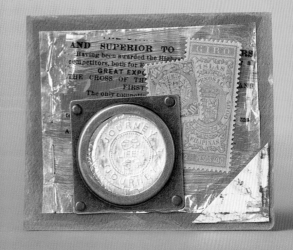

HAWAII: by Kelly Anderson
Supplies *Mesh:* Ink It!; *Dimensional Adhesive:* Diamond Glaze, JudiKins; *Other:* Travel memorabilia.

idea to note: A coat of glaze can add shine and serve as a decoupage medium for travel memorabilia.

"S": by Miley Johnson
Supplies *Canvas:* Hancock Fabrics; *Ribbon:* Memory Lane; *Color wash:* Adirondack, Ranger Industries; *Stencil:* Office Depot; *Brad:* Making Memories; *Other:* Tag.

idea to note: Custom color canvas by spraying it with a color wash. Walnut ink can also be used to add a rich color to plain tags.

ANY TIME ✦ ✦ ✦

R I D E

✦ ✦ ANY WEATHER

Where there's a bike, there's a way. This seems to be the mantra of the Johnson boys this summer. We have had soo much rain, you would think we have moved to Seattle, but this has not stopped you guys from sneaking outside to putter and pedal around on those bikes. It must be a guy thing. I certainly don't think I would enjoy getting soaked just to pedal around in a circle, but you guys eat it up..you love every minute of the tour de Omaha. I love this picture. It shows just how content you are in the elements of nature. Rain or shine, you are outdoor boys ready to roll..or pedal..or run...which ever suits your fancy.

2004

RIDE: by Miley Johnson

Supplies *Patterned paper:* Chatterbox; *Computer font:* Hours, downloaded from the Internet; *Tiles:* Junkitz; *Alphabet stamps:* PSX Design; *Stamping ink:* StazOn, Tsukineko; *Rub-ons and embroidery floss:* Making Memories; *Washers:* Lowe's; *Other:* Canvas, dye and brads.

idea to note: To create colored twill, mask with duct tape and hand dye the canvas with a small toothbrush. Allow to dry, then remove the tape. White acrylic tiles can be recolored using the dye, as well.

inspiration from outside sources

Sometimes ideas appear when you least expect them. If you study the world around you with a scrapbooker's eye, you'll find fascinating details that can inspire attention-grabbing accents for future layouts. Here are a few examples:

purses and totes. Many manufacturers include logo tags with their bags. Everything from leather-embossed frames to metal charms to sewn canvas shapes—bags may also feature innovative closures, funky snaps or interesting pockets.

key chains. Souvenir-style key chains are manufactured in a variety of eye-catching metals, materials, colors and shapes. Most are good models of dimension, texture, shakers and tags.

shoes. Several sandals and strappy slides are topped with pretty flowers, buckles, studs and beading.

fashion accessories. Bracelets, belts, rings, necklaces and earrings feature funky charms, tokens, buckles, tags and ties.

YOU MAKE ME SMILE: by Miley Johnson
Supplies *Fabric:* Frazzles; *Flash card:* Mantofev; *Charm frames:* Sears Portrait Studio; *Alphabet stamps:* PSX Design.

idea to note: A vintage flash card can become a pocket to hold small photos. Use ribbon to string charm frames across it as a pretty adornment.

FOLLOW YOUR BLISS: by Denise Pauley
Supplies *Terra Cotta paste:* Delta Technical Coatings; *Alphabet stamps:* Hero Arts; *Stamping ink:* StazOn, Tsukineko; *Flower punch:* 2Grrrls; *Snap:* Making Memories; *Beaded chain:* American Tag Co.; *Other:* Key.

idea to note: For a realistic "brick" look, brush cardstock with terra cotta texture paint, then hand cut rectangles. Round the corners and aim for a little natural imperfection.

A PERFECT DAY: by Nichol Magouirk
Supplies *Patterned paper:* Design Originals; *Frame:* Upon A Charm; *Butterfly:* K & Company; *Metallic rub-ons:* Craf-T Products; *Paint, safety pin and tag:* Making Memories; *Fixative:* Krylon.

idea to note: When applying metallic rub-ons to a metal frame, first brush the frame with acrylic paint and let it dry to give the rub-ons a surface to stick to.

ALL BOY: by Joy Uzarraga
Supplies: *Fabric, button and cardboard:* Junkitz.

idea to note: Fabric isn't just for girls! Use strips with cool colors to create accents for boy pages. *(Note:* Be resourceful. To create a tag, use cardboard from the fabric packaging and pull threads from the fabric strips to tie on a button.)